Gallery Books
Editor: Peter Fallon

RACINE'S PHAEDRA

Derek Mahon

RACINE'S PHAEDRA

Gallery Books

Racine's Phaedra
is first published
simultaneously in paperback
and in a clothbound edition
on 6 February 1996.

The Gallery Press
Loughcrew
Oldcastle
County Meath
Ireland

ISBN 1 85235 165 9 (*paperback*)
    1 85235 166 7 (*clothbound*)

Racine's Phaedra was commissioned by the Gate Theatre, Dublin.
    The Gallery Press receives financial assistance from An Chomh-
airle Ealaíon / The Arts Council, Ireland, and acknowledges also
the assistance of the Arts Council of Northern Ireland in the publi-
cation of this book.

Characters

PHAEDRA, wife of Theseus, daughter of Minos and Pasiphaë
THESEUS, King of Athens
HIPPOLYTUS, son of Theseus and Antiope
ARICIA, Athenian princess
THERAMENES, Hippolytus' tutor
OENONE, Phaedra's nurse
ISMENE, Aricia's friend
PANOPE, a young woman of Phaedra's circle

Racine's Phaedra opened at the Gate Theatre, Dublin, on 6 February 1996 with the following cast:

PHAEDRA	Dearbhla Molloy
THESEUS	Michael Byrne
HIPPOLYTUS	Stephen Kennedy
ARICIA	Siobhán Miley
THERAMENES	Gerard McSorley
OENONE	Ingrid Craigie
ISMENE	Catherine Walsh
PANOPE	Gertrude Montgomery

Director	John Crowley
Set and costume design	Giles Cadle
Lighting designer	Alan Burrett

Translator's Note

Jean Racine's *Phèdre* was first performed on 1 January 1677, at the Hôtel de Bourgogne, Paris, with Marie de Champmeslé in the title role. The play has long been considered one of the greatest glories of the French theatre, perhaps the greatest; yet, though Dryden might have made a fair fist of it — as Otway did with *Titus and Berenice* (1677) — no adequate English-language version existed until 1961, when Robert Lowell's appeared. Richard Wilbur's followed in 1986. Tony Harrison's *Phaedra Britannica*, meanwhile, set in India, had some success at the Old Vic, London, in 1975. Whatever the reasons for the long neglect (there is a tradition of Anglophone resistance to French tragedy), *Phèdre* is now considered as a strikingly modern play. The Racinian *huis clos* seems to anticipate certain modern intensities; while his psychological realism and poetic force have been much admired. Lowell, in a prefatory note, 'On Translating Racine', speaks of the 'diamond edge' and 'hard electric rage' of Racine's verse; and the present version tries to give some indication of these qualities in the original.

ACT ONE

The summer palace at Troezene; images of Artemis and Aphrodite to left and right.
   On stage: HIPPOLYTUS, THERAMENES.

HIPPOLYTUS
Theramenes, I've come to a decision:
I'm leaving Troezene immediately.
Considering the doubts that trouble me,
I start to blush at my own indolence.
My father's been gone now six months at least
and we've no knowledge of his whereabouts.

THERAMENES
Where will you look for him, my lord? Already,
to set your mind at rest, we've sent out ships
to scour not only the whole Peloponnese
but the Ionian and Aegean seas
and seek news of the king upon those shores
where Acheron disappears among the shades.
They've called at Paros, Naxos, Mykonos
and even crossed the sea where Icarus drowned.
What makes you think, at this late stage,
that you'll discover him in some happier place?
King Theseus, for reasons of his own,
may wish to keep his whereabouts unknown;
or maybe, while we wait here in suspense,
he spends his time, absorbed in some fresh conquest,
with some unfortunate girl . . .

HIPPOLYTUS
Theramenes, that's enough; show some respect.

11

All that's behind him; nothing of that sort
can be the reason for his prolonged absence.
It's a long time since Phaedra feared a rival.
I'm duty-bound to go, in any case,
and that way I escape this dangerous place.

THERAMENES

Dangerous? When did you begin to fear
this pleasant spot your childhood held so dear
and which I've often known you choose above
the pompous tumult of the Athenian court?
What 'danger' is it prompts your departure?

HIPPOLYTUS

The place is changed; those sweet days are no more
since the gods sent *Phaedra* to this quiet shore.

THERAMENES

I think I understand your difficulties.
Her presence is intolerable in your eyes.
She's dangerous, certainly. Your exile
started the minute she set eyes on you;
but now her hate, once so implacable,
has either vanished or is in remission.
Besides, what can she do to a man like you —
a dying woman, one who wants to die?
Sick of a strange disease she shrouds in secrecy,
sick of herself, sick of the light of day,
she's in no state to scheme against you here.

HIPPOLYTUS

It's not her futile enmity I fear
but the survivor of a troublesome house
that once conspired against us: young Aricia.

THERAMENES

What, do *you* persecute her too, my lord?
She had no knowledge of her brothers' plot.
Don't say you hate her for her lovely face?

HIPPOLYTUS
If hate were what I feel, I wouldn't run away.

THERAMENES
I think I understand you. Can it be
you are no longer that imperious prince
impatient with the constraints of love
the king your father's so enamoured of?
Can it be that Aphrodite, whom you slight,
has proved your amorous father in the right
and, treating you like other mortal men,
forced you to light your incense at her shrine?
Are you in love?

HIPPOLYTUS
How can you ask, old friend,
you who have known me since I was a boy?
Do you expect me shamefully to disown
the principles of a heart as proud as mine?
The pride you remark upon is not only
inherited from an Amazonian mother
but derives also from a recognition
of my own value, now that I'm of age.
Don't you remember how, when I was young,
you used to tell me stories about my father?
Don't you remember how I listened, rapt,
to your descriptions of his heroic deeds
and exploits, worthy of great Hercules,
of villains slain and monsters choked to death
— Procrustes, Periphetes, Cercyon in their gore,
the giant's bones scattered at Epidaurus,
Crete smoking from the defeated Minotaur?
Don't you remember how reluctantly
I heard your stories of less glorious deeds,
of pledges given and broken everywhere —
Helen seduced from her parental home,
Periboea in tears at Salamis
and others whose very names he has forgotten —
Ariadne venting her sorrows to the rocks;
Phaedra, last but not least, abducted too!

Don't you remember how, hearing these things,
I'd beg you to cut short your narrative,
anxious to erase the painful facts
casting their shadow on more glorious acts.
So is it my turn now to compromise
my independence with new thoughts of love?
How can I be in love? I have no string
of honours to give weight to such a thing
as my brave father has. So far, at least,
I have no stricken monsters to my credit
to mitigate a sentimental weakness.
Even were I to lose my independence,
would I be mad enough to choose Aricia?
Do you imagine I could be so far gone
as to forget the obstacles between us?
My father has forbidden her to marry
and create nephews for her seditious brothers;
so fearful is he of their treacherous line
he aims to keep her in his own protection
and bury the name with her eventually.
No nuptial fires for her. Do you suppose
I'm eager to adopt Aricia's cause?
I can just see us sail off into the sunset!

THERAMENES

When once it happens and your hour is nigh
the gods aren't interested in your sophistry.
Theseus, wishing to shut your eyes, has opened them;
his opposition, kindling a wild flame,
lends a new charm to his old enemy.
But why be frightened of a real emotion?
Do you still cling to your harsh isolation?
Even the bravest men have fallen in love.
Where would you be now if Antiope,
your mother, hadn't loved King Theseus?
And why put on a show of noble scorn?
Admit it, you are a changed man; these days
we seldom see you, violent and sure,
racing your chariot along the shore.
No longer echoing to your hunting horn,

the woods are quieter than of yore;
consumed with a secret fire, your eyes avoid my gaze.
There's no doubt about it, you're in love;
you try to hide it but the signs are there.

HIPPOLYTUS

Theramenes, please; I'm off to find my father.

THERAMENES

Won't you see Phaedra before you go?

HIPPOLYTUS

I suppose I must; duty requires I do.
But what fresh grief afflicts her dear Oenone?

Enter OENONE.

OENONE

Alas, my lord, what grief is worse than mine?
The queen is in a frightening decline.
Sitting beside her for three nights and days,
I've watched her suffer from an unknown disease.
She starves herself, her spirit is in turmoil.
Some restless misery drives her from her bed
in search of daylight; but her wretchedness
is such that I daren't let her show her face.

HIPPOLYTUS

Of course; I understand. I'll leave her here
and take my hated countenance elsewhere.

Exeunt HIPPLOYTUS *and* THERAMENES; *enter* PHAEDRA.

PHAEDRA

Let's go no farther, dear Oenone; stop!
I can't go on; my strength has left me.
The light dazzles my eyes
and my knees shake as if they would collapse.

OENONE
The gods relieve you of your miseries!

PHAEDRA
This finery only adds to my distress.
What busy hands have done my hair like this?
Everything conspires to increase my woe.

OENONE
Your wishes contradict each other so!
Just now you had us help you look your best
when, gathering strength, it was your firm desire
to show yourself and see the light once more.
Here is the light, madame; and now you cower,
hating the light you've just been asking for!

PHAEDRA
Great sun, the source of our unhappy line,
whom even Pasiphaë was proud to own,
perhaps you blush for me in my affliction?
I come to gaze on you for the last time.

OENONE
Oh, please renounce this desperate design.
Tell me, how much longer do you propose
to go on making these dismal preparations?

PHAEDRA
If I could hide myself in a dark forest
and watch from there, in a thick cloud of dust,
a lonely chariot at the water-line . . .
Where am I? What am I babbling about, Oenone?
Heaven has deprived me of my reason;
I'm so ashamed of my humiliation
and yet I can't seem to restrain my tears.

OENONE
If you must weep, weep for the secrecy
which only aggravates your misery.
Rejecting our concern and deaf to argument,

do you intend to die without a fight?
Why think of dying when you're still so young?
What monstrous poison has dried up the spring?
Three days and nights you've struggled through since last
you had a wink of sleep or broke your fast.
What right have you to trifle with your life?
You wrong the gods who placed you on this earth;
you wrong your husband who believes in you;
you wrong your children, finally, and cast
terrible burdens on them for the future;
for, on the same day you abandon them,
hope will inspire another woman's son,
your enemy and the enemy of your line —
I mean your stepson, young Hippolytus.

PHAEDRA

Oh, God!

OENONE

    Do my words strike home?

PHAEDRA

             Whose name was
that you spoke?

OENONE

Your righteous anger comes as a relief;
I'm happy you can still react like this.
If love and duty fire you, you will live
lest this ambitious Scythian dispossess
your son, establish his own rule in Greece
and lord it over our superior race.
No more dithering; you'll destroy yourself.
It's time now to take charge of your own life.
Call quickly now on your remaining strength
while hope still smoulders and may yet revive.

PHAEDRA

My guilty life has lasted long enough.

OENONE

Guilt? What remorse is eating at you? What
reason have you to feel remorse? What grounds?
There is no innocent blood upon your hands?

PHAEDRA

Thanks be to God, my hands are innocent.
I only wish my thoughts were equally so.

OENONE

What awful notion have you dreamt up,
so terrible you yourself are scared of it?

PHAEDRA

I've said too much and I will say no more;
I'd rather die than let the truth be known.

OENONE

Die if you must, and keep your mysteries,
but look for someone else to close your eyes.
Even though your light grows dim and all but fades
I shall go down before you to the shades.
A thousand paths await us night and day
and, in my grief, I'll find the shortest way.
When have I ever let you down?
For you I left my family and my home.
Are these the thanks I get for all I've done?

PHAEDRA

What do you hope to gain by violence?
You'd die of horror if I broke my silence.

OENONE

Nothing could be worse than to stand aside
while you commit this gradual suicide.

PHAEDRA

When I reveal the fate that crushes me
I'll die no less, but die more guiltily.

OENONE

Madam, deliver me from suspicion;
tell me, for heaven's sake, what's going on.

PHAEDRA

I want to; but I don't know where to start.

OENONE

These vague fears wound me to the heart.

PHAEDRA

To be love's victim is a terrible fate;
think of Pasiphaë's unnatural crime.

OENONE

Forget these ancient histories; and let
the memory be erased till the end of time.

PHAEDRA

Ariadne, my sister, another victim lost
and left to weep alone on a rocky coast.

OENONE

What is it now? What special misery
makes you drag up your whole unfortunate family?

PHAEDRA

Since heaven intends it, I shall die in turn,
the last and the most piteous of my line.

OENONE

Are you in love with a man?

PHAEDRA
    Violently.

OENONE
            With whom?

PHAEDRA

I can't quite bring myself to speak his name.
You know the severity I've shown the son
of Theseus' first wife, the Amazon?

OENONE

Hippolytus? My God!

PHAEDRA

The very same.

OENONE

Sweet heaven, the thought turns my blood to ice.
Must the misfortunes of Pasiphaë
and Ariadne fall upon you too?
Why did we come here to this treacherous place?

PHAEDRA

The trouble started earlier; scarcely had I
emerged 'radiant' from my wedding ceremony,
my fondest hopes apparently fulfilled,
when there, in Athens, stood this haughty prince.
I saw him, blushed, and paled beneath his glance,
knowing right then and there my fate was sealed.
My eyes no longer saw, I couldn't speak,
I felt my body freeze and burn at once.
I recognized the hand of Aphrodite
from whose effect there's no immunity
and, hoping to deflect her fierce attention,
ordered a temple in her honour where,
absorbed in sacrifice, I would inspect
entrails for my disheveled self-respect —
a poor expedient for incurable love!
My hands burned incense at her shrine in vain
for, even as my lips called on the goddess' name,
it was the austere prince that I invoked.
Seeing him everywhere, even in the altar-smoke,
I offered up my soul to a mere man.
I strove to avoid him but, to my distress,
he seemed to stare out of his father's face.

I forced myself, eventually, to work
against him, and insisted on his banishment.
I simulated a stepmother's dislike,
shrieked for his exile till my tedious rage
estranged him from his father; then at last
I breathed again. With him out of the way,
I lived more easily from day to day.
Faithful to Theseus, hiding my despair,
I devoted myself to the children; however
denial was in vain. Re-settled here
by my own husband, in the Peloponnese,
I met again the foe I'd fled before
and here my wound re-opened. Now no more
is the love-fever confined to my veins alone;
love clings like a predator to flesh and bone.
I look with horror on my own transgression,
I hate my life and its illicit passion.
I had hoped death would keep my honour bright
and save my dark devotion from the light;
now, yielding to your insistence and your tears,
I've told you everything, and I'm glad I have —
provided you stop torturing my ears
with vain reproaches, trying to make me live.

    Enter PANOPE.

PANOPE
I wish it were otherwise, madam, but I bring
bad news: death has deprived us of the king,
your husband. You are the last one to know.

PHAEDRA
What do you tell me, Panope? Is this true?

PANOPE
It's been confirmed; the ships are back in port
and have provided a first-hand report.

PHAEDRA
              My God!

Athens, they say, is divided on the issue
of a successor. Some support your son
while others, disregarding the constitution,
have given their voices to Hippolytus;
it's even said that an extreme faction
wishes to place Aricia on the throne.
I thought I ought to warn you of these trends.
Hippolytus sails immediately for Athens —
where, in the present confusion,
he may well stage a palace revolution.

OENONE

Thank you, Panope, for your information.

Exit PANOPE.

My dear, I'd ceased to hope that you might live.
I'd even thought to follow you, since I
no longer had my old influence on your heart;
but this fresh blow dictates another start.
Your luck has changed; and now, with the king gone,
you must replace him. Think of your own son,
a slave if you should die, a king if you should win.
Who could he turn to in the event of your death?
Who else is there he could rely upon?
The gods, his ancestors, listening to his grief,
will curse you that you took your life.
You've nothing to be ashamed of now, so live;
you've now no reason not to declare your love.
With the king dead, the whole knot is untied
that made you think in terms of suicide.
Hippolytus you need no longer fear
and you may see him now without censure;
moreover if, convinced of your aversion,
he indeed aims to start a revolution,
show him his error and restrain his pride,
let him have Troezene and its countryside;
he knows the law bestows Minerva's own
city of Athens on your son alone.

This will sound strange coming from me:
You might combine your forces, you and he,
against Aricia's treacherous coterie.

PHAEDRA

So be it, I'll live on as you suggest
if life will still accept my anorexic ghost
and if a mother's love can still reclaim
my weakened spirits at this difficult time.

Exeunt PHAEDRA and OENONE; enter ARICIA and
ISMENE.

ARICIA

Hippolytus has asked to see me here?
He seeks me out in order to take leave?
Are you quite sure there's no mistake, Ismene?

ISMENE

This is the first effect of Theseus' death.
Expect to notice now on every side
the love and trust he took from you revive.
At last you are the mistress of your fate;
quite soon you will see Athens at your feet.

ARICIA

It's not some baseless rumour?
I am no longer outcast, no longer in disgrace?

ISMENE

The gods are no longer against you
now Theseus' shade has joined your brothers' shades.

ARICIA

Do we know how he died?

ISMENE

Incredible stories have been circulating.
Some say he died in character, resisting
the vengeful onrush of Cocytus' water,

having proposed to rape great Ceres' daughter,
Persephone, on that forsaken shore.
He'd been exploring in the underworld
and shown himself alive among the dead —
from whence, of course, forbidden to depart,
he never found his way back to the light.

ARICIA

I can't believe a living man would choose
to visit the underworld deliberately;
was this some drug-induced hallucination?

ISMENE

Theseus is dead; you alone doubt the thing.
Athens mourns; and Troezene, hearing of it,
already hails Hippolytus as king.
Phaedra, here in the palace, anxious for her son,
confers already with her advisers.

ARICIA

Do you think Hippolytus will be less severe
than Theseus, ease our situation here
and be more merciful?

ISMENE

I believe so, yes.

ARICIA

But don't you know what a cold fish he is?
What makes you think he'll take pity on me,
he who is famous for his misogyny?
You must have noticed how he avoids our sight
and orders things so that we never meet.

ISMENE

I know what they say about his arrogance
but I've observed this proud prince in your presence
when, bearing in mind his haughty reputation,
I watched him with particular attention;
and I must say his manner, when you met,

was not at all what I'd been led to expect.
I saw him grow confused; try as he might,
he couldn't stop staring at you. No doubt
he takes a dim view of women; but his eyes
express things his intolerant heart denies.

ARICIA

How eagerly I listen to what you say
even if there's no truth in it. Ismene,
you know me. Do you think it possible
that I, the victim of a gratuitous fate,
nourished on tears and bitterness,
might know the trivial miseries of love?
The last descendant of Erectheus,
a king once, I alone have survived the war
that saw my brothers cut down in their flower,
the youthful hope of our illustrious line.
The sword reaped, and the moist earth drank down
the hot blood of Erectheus' progeny.
You know, since that day, Theseus' decree
prescribes absolute celibacy for me
lest, giving birth to sons, I should revive
my brothers' names and keep their cause alive;
but you know too with what a contemptuous eye
I've viewed the fears of our vigilant adversary
and how it suited my own disposition
to be subject to such a prohibition;
you know my secret gratitude that Theseus'
harshness reinforced my inclination —
this at a time before I'd seen his son!
Not that I love only the young man's handsomeness,
his famous beauty and his physical grace,
mere natural gifts he probably despises
or whose very existence he scarcely realizes.
No, what I prize in him is something else,
his father's qualities without his faults;
and I admit I prize the fine reserve
which makes him look askance at sexual love.
What pride can Phaedra know as Theseus' wife?
I, for one, think more highly of myself

than to be satisfied with a factitious ardour
offered to others many times before,
and a heart hospitable as an open door.
Ah, but to tame an independent spirit,
to sow confusion in a stony heart,
to see the startled look in his eyes
when, to his pleasure and surprise,
he finds that his is a vain resistance —
that's what excites me about the young prince,
a harder conquest still
than Hercules who, though strong, was vulnerable.
Ismene dear, how can I dare to boast?
The very qualities I look up to most
may be the ruin of me, and you may hear
me groan under the pride I now admire.
Hippolytus in love? What dream is this?

ISMENE
Well, we shall soon know; for here he is.

Enter HIPPOLYTUS.

HIPPOLYTUS
I've come because I wanted you to know
what lies in store for you, before I go.
The king is dead. My worst fears, based
on his long absence, have been justified —
whom only death, closing a great career,
could keep so long from his commitments here.
The gods have given up to murderous fate
Hercules' friend and heir. Despite your hate,
perhaps even you will recognize
the virtues and the achievements which were his.
One thought alleviates my mortal grief —
I can, at last, offer you some relief,
revoking a harsh law which never had my support.
Dispose your heart and hand as you see fit;
for here in Troezene, once the domain
of my grandfather, and where I now reign,
you are at liberty — more so than I.

ARICIA

You're too kind; can your generosity
release me from your father's interdiction?

HIPPOLYTUS

Athens, uncertain where to place the crown,
speaks of yourself, of me, and of Phaedra's son.

ARICIA

Of me, my lord?

HIPPOLYTUS

Of you. A discriminatory
Athenian statute seems to void my claim
because my mother wasn't born in Greece.
If my half-brother were my only rival
I have a genuine precedence over him
which should protect me from the law's caprice.
I yield, though, to a stronger claim: your own.
I yield, or rather give you back, a throne
rightfully yours by reason of descent
from great Erectheus, first son of Earth.
Athens was happy to crown Theseus
and leave your brothers in oblivion;
but now, exhausted by recurrent crises,
recalls you to her hospitable hearth.
Greece has seen too much war, too much random
atrocity disfiguring the kingdom
where life steams from the fields that gave it birth,
and cries aloud to heaven for some relief.
Troezene is mine, and the wide plains of Crete
offer to Phaedra's son a rich retreat.
Athens is yours; I go now to combine
in your own name her factions, yours and mine.

ARICIA

I'm baffled and amazed by what I hear —
and fearful, almost, lest it be a dream.
Am I awake? Dare I believe my ears?
It's some god inspires these plans of yours.

How rightfully the world extols your merit,
and how the truth itself exceeds report!
You'd really back my claim against your own?
Is it not enough that you don't hate me
or let your heart be ruled by enmity . . .

HIPPOLYTUS

Hate you? I know I'm thought aloof and grim;
but I'm no monster, no fierce minotaur.
What savage heart, what violent character
would not, to look at you, grow amiable?
Could I resist such a beguiling charm?

ARICIA

What are you saying, sir?

HIPPOLYTUS

      I've gone too far.
Reason fails where love is in the balance;
for, now that I've begun to break my silence,
I must go on to tell you a secret
I can no longer lock up in my heart.
You see before you a deplorable prince,
a fine example of blind arrogance.
I who, contemptuous of the emotional life,
despised the victims of its amorous strife
and, pitying lesser mortals' turmoil, swore
always to watch their shipwrecks from the shore,
now find myself a victim like the rest,
my ship blown from its course by the same tempest!
One glance destroyed my frivolous self-control;
obedience reigns in my hubristic soul.
These last six months, ashamed and desperate,
I've trailed around the shaft that tears my heart,
wrestling with you and with my own despair.
I shun you and I find you everywhere.
Your face confronts me even in the darkest wood;
daylight and night-time, both, combine to flood
my brain with images I can't ignore;
all things conspire to place me in your power.

Resistance is in vain; turn where I will
your cold prince is unrecognizable.
My usual pastimes are of little interest
nor do I ride out now with the same zest;
my hunters, idle now, no longer know
my voice, and the woods echo only to my woe.
You blush, I see, at my crude declaration
to think yourself the cause of such uncouth devotion.
What a rough offer of my love I make;
what a rough prisoner does your beauty take!
All the more reason, though, to take me seriously;
remember, this is a foreign tongue to me —
and don't rebuff my words, however broken,
which, but for you, would never have been spoken.

Enter THERAMENES.

THERAMENES

My lord, the queen has sent me on to say
she's coming here to see you right away.

HIPPOLYTUS

                                    What, me?

THERAMENES

I don't know why, but I'm to let you know
she needs to speak to you before you go.

HIPPOLYTUS

Phaedra? What have we got to talk about?

ARICIA

Sir, you mustn't refuse to hear her out.
Even if she seems your enemy for life,
you must, at least, respect her widowed grief.

HIPPOLYTUS

But now you'll leave me, and I'm leaving too
not knowing how my words have influenced you,
not knowing how you take my declaration.

ARICIA

Go, prince, pursue your generous line of action
and reassure Athens in my regard.
Of course I accept everything you've offered;
yet these estates, so great, so glorious,
are not the dearest of your gifts to us.

Exeunt ARICIA *and* ISMENE.

HIPPOLYTUS

All set, old friend? . . . Oh God, look, here she comes!
We leave immediately. Go quick, prepare
the ships for our departure;
then get back here at once
and interrupt this tedious conference.

Exit THERAMENES; *enter* PHAEDRA and OENONE.

PHAEDRA

There he is; my heart races. Seeing him here today
I don't remember what I meant to say.

OENONE

Think of your *own* son; you are his only chance.

PHAEDRA

My lord, I'm told you're leaving us at once,
and so I've come to share your desolation
and tell you of my fears for my own son.
He has no father now; and it won't be long
before he also finds his mother gone.
Already numerous enemies seek to exploit
his inexperience. You can help him; though
I'm quite aware my previous persecution
may well have shut your ears to our petition.
I hate to think how my poor boy might suffer
from your just fear of his obnoxious mother.

HIPPOLYTUS

Rest assured; I have no such thing in mind.

PHAEDRA

If you should hate me, I would understand.
You've often seen me try to harm you, though
my secret thoughts were not for you to know.
I took care to incur your enmity
and banish you from my vicinity;
I worked against you, asking nothing more
than space between us; I even went so far,
by special edict, as to proclaim
that no one, in my presence, speak your name.
You hate me, naturally; yet if you could see
the unhappiness your hate creates in me,
you'd know no woman more deserves your pity
or less deserves your animosity.

HIPPOLYTUS

A mother, anxious for her children's rights,
rarely forgives the son of the first wife.
I know it; and what maddening suspicion
remarriage breeds. Others in your position,
no doubt, would have felt similarly towards me
and perhaps acted even more venomously.

PHAEDRA

God, if you only knew how wrong you are
and the true source and nature of my despair!

HIPPOLYTUS

Even now the king may be upon the sea,
madame; we may have heard a false report.
Heaven may yet return him safe to port.
Poseidon minds him; and the king won't cry
in vain upon his guardian deity.

PHAEDRA

No one walks twice among the dead below.
Since Theseus set his foot on those dark shores,
you hope in vain some god will show remorse;
for Acheron never lets its victim go.
. . . What am I saying? He is not dead and gone;

31

I see him when I look at you, his son.
I see him, speak to him, and my bursting heart . . .
But my love cries aloud when it should be mute.

HIPPOLYTUS
Madam, your faith is truly admirable;
dead though he be, you see great Theseus still.

PHAEDRA
I thirst for Theseus; though the one I mean
is not the Theseus the dead have seen,
the ravenous lover of a thousand women
intent on raping great Persephone, even —
but serious, proud, even a little fierce,
handsome and young, breaking hearts everywhere
as we depict our gods, or as I see you there.
He had your very presence, look and voice,
it was your fine reserve coloured his face
when once upon a time he came to Crete
to find King Minos' daughters at his feet.
And where were you, young man, when the elite
of Grecian heroism assembled there?
Though just a boy, you might have slipped aboard
one of the ships that brought them to our shore.
You might have been the one to liquidate
the monster in its labyrinth. My late
sister might have equipped *you* with a ball
of string to guide you from the maze; or, better still,
I'd be the one to take the initiative;
love would have put the thought into my head.
It would have been *my* guiding hand that gave
instruction in the secrets of the cave.
What wouldn't I have done to save my love?
A thread would not have been enough. A thread?
We would have gone down where your courage led
with Phaedra out in front! Down there together,
we would have lost and found ourselves forever.

HIPPOLYTUS
Think what you're saying, ma'am. Have you forgotten

that you are Theseus' wife, and I his son?

PHAEDRA
Forgotten? What do you think? Do you imagine
I have no care for my own reputation?

HIPPOLYTUS
I misinterpreted your . . . 'fantasy' —
and I apologize. Now, if you'll excuse me . . .

PHAEDRA
Ah, cruel prince, you understood me perfectly;
I've said enough to make my meaning plain.
So here stands Phaedra, obviously insane,
who loves you; and, though innocent enough,
don't think me happy in my furious love
or that a weak compliance of my own
has fed the poison eating up my brain.
A wretched victim of celestial spite,
my self-hatred exceeds even your hate.
The gods, who lit the hot fire in my thigh
that scorches all my kin, could tell you why —
those very gods who, on a sadistic whim,
destroy mere mortal hearts for sport. No doubt
you can recall to mind our past relations,
my various coldnesses and persecutions.
I wished to appear odious, to frustrate
my love, and sought to cultivate your hate.
A stupid tactic; for, as your hatred grew,
so my unprofitable love grew too.
Adversity increased your fascination;
I pined and wasted, between storms and sighs.
You'd appreciate this reckless declaration
if you could bear to look me in the eyes.
What am I saying? Do you think it's fun
making a spectacle of myself like this?
I came in fear to speak for my *own* son
lest he should suffer for my past behaviour
— a foolish notion in the circumstances —
and rave on about *you* is all I've done.

Avenge yourself, punish my hideous love.
True son of Theseus, rid the radiant earth
of one more monster perilous to its peace!
Theseus' widow dares to love his son?
A beast like that deserves to perish! Look,
here is my breast, here's where your hand should strike!
Eager to expiate its guilt, my black
heart goes out to meet your hand; so strike!
Strike! Do you refuse?
Am I unworthy of your blows?
Will you not stain your hands with tainted blood?
I'll do it myself; here, give me your sword.

> *She seizes his sword.* OENONE *wrests it from her hands.*
> *It falls to the ground, where it remains.*

OENONE
Heavens above, you can't be seen like this!
We must leave here at once to avoid disgrace.

Exeunt PHAEDRA *and* OENONE; *enter* THERAMENES.

THERAMENES
Was that Phaedra I saw rushing away?
. . . You seem stricken, my lord;
won't you confide in me? And where's your sword?

HIPPOLYTUS
Let's go, Theramenes; I am greatly shaken
and don't feel very pleased with myself right now.
Phaedra . . . No, I can't speak of it;
this thing must remain secret and unspoken.

THERAMENES
The ships are ready when you wish to sail.
Athens, however, has announced its choice.
The constituencies have spoken with one voice
and chosen Phaedra's son; so they prevail.

HIPPOLYTUS

Phaedra?

THERAMENES
                Yes, a communiqué from Athens
places the reins of government in her hands.
She rules until her first-born comes of age.

HIPPOLYTUS
I expect it's her moral character the gods wish to
    acknowledge.

THERAMENES
Meanwhile there's a rumour the king's re-appeared
in Ithaca; I'll have inquiries made, but . . .

HIPPOLYTUS
                                            Leave no stone
    unturned.
Trace it back to its source; and should it prove
too slight to keep us here, we'll leave
and stop at nothing now to place
a *fit* successor on the throne of Greece.

Exeunt; enter PHAEDRA *and* OENONE.

PHAEDRA
I can't go through with any kind of ceremony.
How can I face the world in this condition?
And don't try to relieve my desolation.
Better you hid me; I have said too much.
My furies have escaped and shrieked abroad,
proclaiming things that never should be heard.
Oh, how he listened! How disingenuously
the ruffian strove to misinterpret me!
How frantically he wriggled to get clear,
his irritation adding to my despair!
And you — why block the deliverance I desired?
When I had almost fallen upon his sword,
was he afraid for me? How did he respond?

It was enough I'd touched it,
spoiling its masculine virtue.
The unfortunate blade would have defiled his hand!

OENONE

Your fury fans a flame you must subdue;
there are more urgent problems facing you.
At this point, would it not be more appropriate
to give some thought to the future of the state?
Forget this prim misogynist; instead
concentrate on the work that lies ahead.

PHAEDRA

I, concentrate? I, run a government
when I no longer govern my own heart?
I, give thought to political events
when I've renounced the sovereignty of sense?
When I am dying?

OENONE

You must leave here.

PHAEDRA

I can't go.

OENONE

You banished him before; can't you avoid him now?

PHAEDRA

It's too late now, after what happened here.
I've outraged decency. I've gone too far;
yet, even as I blurted out my secret,
hope, despite me, crept into my heart.
It was you, rescuing me from certain death
when my mouth trembled with its dying breath,
revived me with your impractical suggestion
and made me think my love legitimate.

OENONE

My dear, guilty or not of your misfortune,

36

for your sake there's nothing I wouldn't do;
but if an insult ever angered you,
how can you disregard his ill-concealed disdain?
With what indifferent, cold eyes
he watched you shame yourself beneath his gaze!
How hateful his ferocious pride!
Didn't you see the way he looked at you?

PHAEDRA

This pride that bothers you is a youthful trait.
Raised in the woods, he has their savagery
and, educated in the grim laws of nature,
he hears this talk of love for the first time.
Perhaps his arrogance was just surprise
and we exaggerate his barbarities.

OENONE

Remember, a barbarian gave him life.

PHAEDRA

Barbarian, Scythian; yet she was a wife.

OENONE

The boy's renowned for his misogyny.

PHAEDRA

No fear of rivals, then, need bother me.
In any case, you're too late with your criticism;
so minister to my madness, not my reason.
He shows love an impenetrable heart?
Let's aim at some more vulnerable part.
The charms of empire draw him, I suspect;
Athens attracts him, he can't hide the fact.
His ships already point in that direction,
sails flapping in the breeze. Oenone, run
to the shore and stop this confident young man;
blind him with thoughts of an imperial crown.
Oh, let him *have* the damn thing; all I require
is that I be the one to place it there.
Let him fulfil a role that's not for me;

he can teach my son the art of sovereignty
and be a father to him by adoption.
I place both mother and son in his protection.
He'll listen to you; try every means to move him.
Weep and moan; say I'm at death's door;
down on your knees before him and implore —
then come back here
and tell me what the future has in store.

    Exit OENONE; PHAEDRA, *alone.*

Implacable goddess, are you satisfied
with my debasement? Does it go far enough?
Your triumph is complete, your shafts have found their
    mark;
there is no need to leave me in the dark.
But, if you're anxious for a fresh victory,
strike now at a more deliberate enemy.
Hippolytus, scorning your authority,
offers no votive candles at your shrine.
His ears are shut to mention of your name.
Avenge yourself; our causes are the same.
Oh, make him love . . . Oenone, back so soon?

    Re-enter OENONE.

He hates me still? He wouldn't listen to you?

OENONE
Madam, you must forget the whole idea.
Recall yourself to duty; for the king,
whom we thought dead, will very soon be here.
Theseus has docked; his ship is at the pier.
Following Hippolytus, as you told me to,
I saw the people crowding to the port
where a great shout went up to left and right.

PHAEDRA
My husband is alive; I might have known.
Oh, I've been guilty of a disgraceful act.

He is alive; don't underline the fact.
I foresaw this, but you didn't want to hear;
your pleas dispelled my reasonable fear.
I might have died this morning, mourned and proud;
thanks to your counsel, I shall die dishonoured.
God in heaven, what have I done today?
Theseus is coming, Hippolytus at his side.
I shall see the recipient of my self-exposure
watch with what nerve I welcome home his father,
my heart still aching with rejected sighs
and disregarded tears filling my eyes.
Do you think, for Theseus' sake, he might disguise
the secret of my adulterous enterprise,
deceiving both his father and his king?
Can he contain his obvious aversion?
Not that his silence would be any solution.
What wickedness I'm guilty of, I know;
nor am I one of your brazen creatures who,
relaxed in happy promiscuity, pass
through a censorious world as bold as brass.
I know the seriousness of what I've done.
I feel as if each pillar here, each stone
could speak and, bursting to articulate,
need only see my husband to cry out.
Death is the one deliverance from this agony;
and is it such a terrible thing to die?
Death isn't terrible to a disordered mind.
I fear only the name I leave behind:
to my poor boys what a grim legacy!
Olympian descent, on the one hand,
ensures they won't lack courage; on the other,
consider the effect of a mad mother.
There's the result that I most fear,
that one day they'll be told what happened here;
and that, oppressed by such a weight of woe,
neither will stand up straight as he ought to.

OENONE

I pity both of them, and that's for sure.
Never were fears more justified than yours;

but why expose them to unhappiness? Why
proclaim your guilt before posterity?
It's simple: die and it will be believed
you couldn't face the husband you deceived.
Hippolytus, of course, will be relieved
to have your death corroborate *his* version.
What could I do in such a situation?
He would discredit me in an instant;
and then I'd have to watch him gloat and hear
him breathe your fate in every curious ear.
I'd rather be at the bottom of the sea
than have to put up with that; but tell me now,
do you still love him? How does he seem to you?

PHAEDRA

To me he is a monster, one of the worst.

OENONE

So fight back; why concede the victory?
You fear Hippolytus? So accuse him first
— immediately — and of the same crime.
Who will deny it? The facts point to him:
your old resentment, present state of mind,
his sword so opportunely left behind,
your oft-repeated cries warning the king,
even his former exile your own doing!

PHAEDRA

What, me, incriminate an innocent man?

OENONE

I ask only that you listen to my plan.
I'm nervous too, and not without remorse.
I'd rather die a thousand deaths, of course;
but since, without this remedy, you'll perish
and it is your life, above all, I cherish,
I'll speak to Theseus, who will confine
his vengeance to the fresh exile of his son.
Even enraged, a father doesn't cease
to be a father; a light sentence will suffice.

But even if some innocent blood should flow,
that's nothing to lost honour in the world's eyes,
honour too precious ever to compromise.
Whatever honour orders you must do.
Honour takes precedence above everything,
above virtue even; but look, I see the king.

PHAEDRA

I see Hippolytus, in whose insolent stare
I read my certain doom. Proceed
as you think best, I leave it all to you;
in my present state I don't know what to do.

Enter THESEUS, HIPPOLYTUS *and* THERAMENES.

THESEUS

Fate, now relenting after much mishap,
restores me to your arms . . .

PHAEDRA

                    Stop, Theseus, stop!
Don't cheapen these words of love,
words I'm no longer worthy to receive.
You have been wronged; the gods who spared your life
have not, while your were absent, spared your wife.
Please excuse me, I am in no condition . . .

Exeunt PHAEDRA *and* OENONE.

THESEUS

Why am I welcomed in this curious fashion?

HIPPOLYTUS

Only she can explain the situation;
but, if you'll grant an earnest wish of mine,
permit me never to see your wife again.
I've had a shock, and would prefer to quit
any environment that she may inhabit.

THESEUS

You wish to leave us?

HIPPOLYTUS

Sir, I never sought her;
when she came down here, it was you who brought her —
who, leaving, left Aricia and the queen
here on the quiet shore of Troezene
where it was my job to look after them.
What further duties can detain me now?
I've wasted too much of my lazy youth
on the shy creatures of the forest.
May I not leave my vain amusements here
and stain my javelins with some worthier game?
Before you'd reached my age now, more than one
tyrant, more than one monster had known
the weight of your displeasure; and, already,
the celebrated scourge of piracy,
you'd fortified the shores of the two seas
so merchantmen could coast in safety. Hercules,
hearing of your achievements too,
laid down his sword and left the rest to you —
while I, despite your fame, am still unknown;
even my mother's name is greater than my own.
Grant my abilities free rein; place in my charge
the head of any monster still at large
or, rescuing my young days from oblivion,
let an heroic exit prove to everyone,
in Greece and farther afield, I was your son.

THESEUS

What's wrong? What horror, spreading in this place,
scatters my family before my face?
Heavens, if my return is so unpopular,
why wasn't I left upon a distant shore?
I had one friend, Pirithoüs, whose unwise ambition
it was to abduct Persephone, the wife of Tartarus' king.
I helped his dark design, with some regret;
but we were hoodwinked by an angry fate.
Her tyrant husband, taking us by surprise,

42

forced me to watch my friend, with my own eyes,
flung screaming to monsters in their den
that chew the bodies of still-living men.
Me he clapped in a subterranean cave,
a Stygian dungeon stinking like the grave.
After six months, heaven noticing my plight,
I managed to escape into the light
where, ridding the earth of my invidious foe,
I served him up for lunch in his own zoo.
But now, when I return here to embrace
my loved ones where they are gathered in this place;
now when my soul, delivered to the light,
would feast once more upon this longed-for sight,
what do I find? Anxiety and fear,
'loved ones' who seem displeased to have me here.
Touched by the very terror I instil,
I might as well be Tartarus' prisoner still!
Phaedra announces I've been wronged. By whom?
Has no one watched my interests? Has Greece,
where in my time I have performed some service,
provided the malefactor with asylum?
Speak up! No answer? Has my own son
joined with my enemies in some machination?
I must clear up this doubt
that crime and criminal be sorted out
and my unhappy wife explain her troubled state.

    Exit.

HIPPOLYTUS

What did she mean? What do her words portend?
Does the demented Phaedra now intend
to disabuse my father? Heavens above,
how will the king react? This violent 'love'
has spread its poison throughout Theseus' house;
while I myself, in love with his sworn foe —
how changed a son I am, did he but know.
Dark, minatory shapes are everywhere;
yet innocence, they say, need never fear.
I shall consider how best to arouse

my father's sympathy for Aricia,
owning to an attachment even his great
resistance has no power to terminate.

ACT TWO

On stage: THESEUS, OENONE.

THESEUS

Do you swear to tell me the perfidious boy
contrived against me while I was away?
How destiny pursues me! Where to turn?
Is there now no one I can depend upon?
Is this how my affection is paid back?
What a degenerate and shameful trick!
And look (*the sword*): the young scoundrel didn't abstain
from *force*, in the furtherance of his dark design.
I recognize this sword he raised against her,
I gave it to him myself as a keepsake.
Could ties of kinship not restrain the monster?
And why did the queen not speak of this before?
Did she propose to shield the young malefactor?

OENONE

She wished, rather, to shield your manly pride.
Ashamed of her anomalous position,
to be abused in such a hateful fashion,
by her own desperate hand she might have died
and closed a life known for its rectitude
except that, fortunately, I was at her side
and so prevented her when she raised the sword.
Now, both her misery and your confusion
oblige me to explain the situation.

THESEUS

Treason! No wonder he was white with fear!
I saw him shake as he received me here

45

and was astonished by his cold embrace,
his curious silence and a grip like ice.
But tell me, this unnatural desire,
why did it not declare itself before?

OENONE

Oh, but it did, sir. Do you not remember
how once, in Athens, Phaedra would complain?
His attitude displeased her even then.

THESEUS

And here in Troezene it began again?

OENONE

I've told you everything there is to know.
Now, since I hate to leave her on her own,
with your permission, sir, I'll take my leave.

Exit OENONE; *enter* HIPPOLYTUS.

THESEUS

Ah, there he is. Who wouldn't be deceived
to see that manly stride and grave demeanour?
How can the face of an adulterer
shine so with the light of conscience? Where
are the sure signs by which we ought to know
the treacherous heart behind the virtuous show?

HIPPOLYTUS

Why do you frown, my lord? What cloud darkens
    your brow?
Whatever it is, won't you confide in me?

THESEUS

How dare you show yourself in my vicinity?
You should have been struck by lightning years ago
or cut down like the monsters I once slew.
Now that your uncontrollable libido
has sought to force itself upon my spouse,
you dare to show your execrable face,

as if nothing had occurred, here in this house
when you should slink off to some foreign place
where nobody knows the name of Theseus! Go,
and don't provoke me further. It's bad enough
posterity will despise me that I let
such an ignoble offspring see the light
without your *murder* darkening my name
and staining the glorious record of my fame.
Go, and unless you wish to join the list
of rogues who've felt the swift weight of my fist,
be careful, in the future, I don't learn
you've set foot in this country once again.
Go, and be gone forever; quit my sight;
relieve my realm of your detested kite!
And you, Poseidon, if I ever cleaned
the murderous scum of pirates from your shore,
remember how, in gratitude, you swore
to grant my first request. I have refrained.
Even in my dungeon, during the darkest hours,
I never called upon your heavenly powers —
saving, instead, the aid you promised me
to call upon in an extremity.
I call upon it now. Discharge your oath.
I cede this knave to your unstinting wrath.
Visit his treason with condign excess:
I'll know your love by your vindictiveness.

HIPPOLYTUS
(*gasps incredulously*)
I'm charged with some unfilial approach?
This is grotesque, and robs me of all speech.

THESEUS
(*picks up Hippolytus' sword*)
You thought she would keep silent; but look here —
your own sword strips away your smooth veneer.
You should have used it, to compound your crime,
to 'rob her speech' and life at the same time.

HIPPOLYTUS

I don't know why I don't expose this lie.
I ought to tell the truth; but for your sake
I shall say nothing, hoping your love will take
my silence as a token of loyalty.
I beg you, try to control your agitation;
think of my life so far, recall your son.
Small crimes always precede the greater: one
who has once overstepped the bounds, quite soon
will violate all the most sacred ties.
Virtue, like wickedness, ripens by degrees.
One never sees the innocent and shy
corrupted in the twinkling of an eye;
nor can you change a good man at one stroke
to a vile murderer or an incestuous crook.
Raised by a chaste, heroic mother, I
have not disgraced that high heredity;
Theramenes, the wisest in these lands,
has been my tutor since I left her hands.
Now, I don't mean to paint too bright a picture
but, should I lay claim to one virtuous feature,
I think I'm known for my antipathy
to just that vice you now ascribe to me.
It's this my name is known for throughout Greece,
an almost *comical* extreme of virtuousness.
I've seen you smile at my naivety.
My chastity is proverbial, the clear light
of heaven is not more innocent than my heart;
and now I'm practically accused of rape . . . !

THESEUS

Your very pride condemns you, you young pup.
I've got the measure of your famous chastity —
only Phaedra pleases your prurient eye
while your indifferent soul disdains the fire
of any natural love or innocent desire.

HIPPOLYTUS

I think the time has come for me to speak
of an 'innocent desire' you may not like.

48

My true transgression is to be in love
where you forbade it — with the shy Aricia
whose brothers thought to stage a coup d'état.
They lost; but now their sister's won my heart.
I love her, sir, despite your prohibition;
I've given her my allegiance and devotion.

THESEUS

Have you indeed! Oh no, I see your oblique
attempt to clear yourself by a cheap trick.

HIPPOLYTUS

I've shunned her for six months, without success,
and came here anxiously to tell you this.
What words of mine can shake your misconception,
what fearful oath revise your mad fixation?
Let earth, and heaven, and the whole of nature . . .

THESEUS

Scoundrels like you are always quick to swear;
so spare me an intolerable lecture
if that's the best hypocrisy can do.

HIPPOLYTUS

Though it seems false and insincere to you,
Phaedra can vouch for my good character;
and she has more humanity, deep down.

THESEUS

You merely enrage me with your insolent tone.

HIPPOLYTUS

Where am I banished to, and for how long?

THESEUS

Were it beyond the Straits of Hercules
I'd still be too close to your treacheries.

HIPPOLYTUS

Charged as I am with this appalling crime,

what friends will speak for me if you decline?

THESEUS

Go seek your friends among the dispossessed
who praise adultery and applaud incest,
traitors and malcontents without honour or virtue,
the fit companions of a wretch like you.

HIPPOLYTUS

Do you still rave about incest and adultery?
I'll say no more, except to remind you
that Phaedra's mother, indeed all her line,
had more experience of these things than mine.

THESEUS

How dare you speak about the queen like that?
I say, for the last time, out of my sight!

He returns the sword to HIPPOLYTUS.

Don't force me to get tough
and have you thrown out like a common thief.

Exit HIPPOLYTUS; THESEUS, *alone.*

THESEUS

Poor boy, you go now to your certain doom —
Poseidon promised by that Stygian stream
not even the immortals view without a qualm.
A vengeful god pursues you, wretched boy.
I loved you; now, despite your wickedness,
my stomach churns to think how you will die.
You leave me with no choice:
when was a parent more abused than I?
Just gods, who see the grief that weighs me down,
how could I father such an ungrateful son?

Enter PHAEDRA.

PHAEDRA

Theseus, I'm scared; I couldn't help but hear.
I heard you in my apartments and I fear
your words will have some terrible consequence.
If there is still time, spare the prince's life;
pardon your son, I ask it as your wife.
Spare me the sound of his imagined cries
and spare me the eternal grief
of being the cause and author of his demise.

THESEUS

My hands are clean; and yet the traitor dies.
Poseidon owes me this, and you besides.

PHAEDRA

Poseidon? Can your intemperate tirade . . . ?

THESEUS

Don't tell me you're afraid it may be heard
but rather join your angry prayers to mine.
I want to know the details of his crime;
stir up my anger, which I still restrain.
You should have heard the way he spoke of you,
implying your accusations were untrue:
he laughs at you, your charges he denies
and claims he loves *Aricia*, if you please!

PHAEDRA
                              Aricia?

THESEUS

Yes; but I know a cheap trick when I see one.
Let's hope Poseidon acts immediately.
I go now to his shrine
to urge fulfilment of this prayer of mine.

Exit THESEUS; PHAEDRA, *alone.*

PHAEDRA

There he goes . . . My God, can it be true?

Aricia? The news comes like a bolt from the blue.
I ran here with one thought, to save his son,
breaking free of Oenone's grip by force,
and yielded to intolerable remorse.
Who knows how far repentance might have gone?
If not shocked into silence, can I be sure
I wouldn't have babbled out a full disclosure?
Hippolytus is in love, but not with me;
the 'shy' Aricia is the beneficiary!
When he responded to my heartfelt sighs
with that fierce countenance and forbidding eyes,
I thought his nature, icy and inhuman,
resistant equally to *every* woman;
now someone else has tamed his fierce hauteur,
someone else pleases his haughty stare.
Perhaps he has a heart easily led.
If I am the one woman he can't bear,
am I the one to spring to his defence?

Enter OENONE.

Oenone, do you know what I've just heard?

OENONE
No, but to tell the truth I've been dead scared
since you rushed off like that,
thinking you'd blurt out something you'd regret.

PHAEDRA
Oenone, what do you know? I have a rival!
Hippolytus is in love; oh yes, it's true.
This heartless brute no woman could subdue,
who found my passionate tears contemptible,
is tame, submissive, and admits defeat:
we've 'shy' Aricia to thank for it.

OENONE
                    Aricia?

PHAEDRA

Ah, what new pain must I now undergo?
What monstrous torture have I yet to know?
All I've endured, the madness and the fear,
self-pity, rage, humiliation, self-hate,
the insult of rejection, even, were mere
ripples of the approaching storm; for, lo,
they are in love! Oh, how did they deceive me?
When and where have they contrived to meet?
Oenone, you must have known this all along:
why didn't you tell me what was going on?
Were they much seen to seek each other out?
Did they go off into the woods? No doubt.
They would have met without difficulties
and heaven approved the innocence of their sighs.
They would have made love without shame or blame,
each day dawned clear and serene for them;
while I, an outcast in Creation's sight,
hid from the sun and shunned the morning light.
Death was the only god I dared address,
and so I watched in vain for my release.
Nourished on wormwood, bathed in my own tears,
and yet too closely watched in my despairs,
I dared not drown my sorrows at my leisure
but sobbed in secrecy or waived the pleasure,
hiding my panic behind a 'regal' air.

OENONE

Much good will it do them, their romance is over;
they'll meet no more.

PHAEDRA

But they will love forever.
Even as we speak I see them sniggering there
at the queer hag in her malign despair:
despite the exile which will sever them,
they vow to be together just the same.
I can't abide their smug beatitude;
you have to understand my furious need.
Aricia must die; we must arouse

my husband's hatred of her treacherous house.
Nor will a trivial punishment suffice,
for she is guiltier than her brothers were.
Theseus will see the point . . . Am I completely crazy?
I turn to Theseus in my jealousy?
My husband is alive and still I sweat —
for whom? Hippolytus. At the very thought
the hair stands up in horror on my head.
I see now that my crime exceeds the bounds
of vice and perjury; while my murderous hands
long to assuage themselves in innocent blood —
and still I live, a black speck in full view
of the bright sun from whom my line descends.
My grandfather was first among the gods,
my forebears stare down from the sun and clouds.
Where should I hide? Among the dead below?
But, clutching the fatal urn, my father sits
in judgement over the dim souls in those parts.
Oh, how his ghost will look up in surprise
when his own daughter comes before his eyes,
forced to confess to every kind of vice
including some never before known in that place.
Father, what will you say to such a sight?
I can just see you drop the urn in fright;
I can just see you, my inquisitor,
dreaming up some new torture for me there.
Forgive me, a tough goddess haunts our house;
you see her hand in my extremity.
I've known no benefit, unfortunately,
from the attentions of great Aphrodite.
Dogged by self-pity to my final breath,
I yield up my tormented soul to death.

OENONE
Dispel these terrors; you exaggerate.
Consider your mistake in a different light.
You are in love; and who can conquer fate?
A fatal influence holds you in its snare:
is there no precedent for this situation?
Are you the first to suffer in this fashion?

After all, weakness is only human;
accept the destiny of a mortal woman.
The condition you resent was always there.
The gods themselves, with their superior powers,
so sanctimonious about our own desires,
are no strangers to the forbidden fires.

PHAEDRA

Now what pernicious talk is this I hear?
Are you going to pour your poison in my ear
right to the last? You'll be the death of me.
You dragged my sorrow into the light of day,
your pleas encouraged my insane persistence;
I saw the prince only at *your* insistence.
How could you take so much upon yourself,
your evil tongue destroying his young life?
That boy could die if the vindictive god
grant Theseus' reckless prayer. Not one more word,
you monstrous person, you unnatural beast.
Go, leave me to my appointed fate at last.
May heaven reward you in a fitting manner
and may your punishment give pause forever
to those who, like yourself, with weasel words,
flatter the weaknesses of unhappy lords
and urge them down the paths of least resistance,
greasing the axles of intrigue — vile sycophants,
the nastiest gift the gods have given us yet!

Exit PHAEDRA.

OENONE

I've given you my life; are these the thanks I get?

Exit OENONE; *enter* HIPPOLYTUS *and* ARICIA.

ARICIA

How can you play dumb at this critical moment
and leave your father in such frightful torment?
If, despite my tears, you can consent
so readily, it seems, to your own banishment,

then leave me to my solitary life;
but first ensure that you yourself are safe.
Defend your honour from this vile untruth
and force your father to revoke his oath.
There is still time. By what perverse compulsion
do you leave a clear field for Phaedra's version?
Why not enlighten him?

HIPPOLYTUS

What more can I say?
That his wife shamed him while he was away?
Should I humiliate him with the truth?
I've opened up my heart to you alone;
only to the gods and you is the truth known.
See how I love you when I can confide
things that even from myself I wished to hide!
Remember though, I beg you, not a word
to a soul about this sordid episode.
We can rely upon the gods' good faith;
they're honour-bound to vindicate myself.
Sooner or later Phaedra will be arraigned
and pay for her deception in the end.
Discretion is the one thing, at this stage,
I ask; aside from that, a bracing rage
absolves me from constraint. And you, my dear,
throw off the servitude of your present plight;
come with me, be a partner in my flight.
Shake off the dust of this unwholesome sphere
where virtue breathes only a poisonous air.
To hide your disappearance, take advantage
of the confusion my disgrace creates.
Don't fret; your safety I can guarantee —
I've spoken to the guards and they're with me.
Powerful friends will rally to our side,
Argos' and Sparta's gates are open wide;
so let's present these allies with our case
lest Phaedra, profiting from our disgrace,
frustrate our expectations and pass on
to her son my just entitlements and your own.
The time is right and we must act at once.

Why do you hesitate? I sense resistance.
It's zeal on your behalf inspires this sacrifice.
Here am I, hot for action, and you as cold as ice.

Believe me, I would welcome an exile such as that.
I'd gladly share with you that happy state,
forgotten by the world and wedded to your fate;
but, not being linked by any formal tie,
how can I decently run off with you?
I'd disregard the king's authority,
I know, without compunction; it's not as though
I've loving parents here; and tyranny
makes escape more or less obligatory.
You love me, so you say; but all the same . . .

No, no, I care too much for your good name.
I've come to you with a more honourable offer:
marry me and we'll leave this place together.
Free in distress, since heaven wills it thus,
we need no king or priest to marry us,
no gongs or torchlight, ceremonial rooms.
Off the Mycenae road, among the tombs
of my ancestors, the princes of our line,
there stands a temple sacred to the truth
where nobody dare swear an oath in vain.
Those who deceive are punished there and then
and liars, fearful of a sudden death,
hold their tongues and save their breath.
There, if you trust me, we will pledge our faith
and our eternal love, asking the god
to act as priest and father to us both;
and there invoke the names we revere most,
chaste Artemis and Juno the august —
though the whole pantheon, indeed,
will vouch for the solemnity of my trust.

Here comes the king; you'd better go. To cloak

57

my own departure, I'll delay a little.
Go on; and send someone reliable
so I can find you when I've finished here.

Exit HIPPOLYTUS; *enter* THESEUS *and* ISMENE.

THESEUS
Into my troubled mind, you gods, throw light!

ARICIA
Ismene, finish here; prepare for flight.

Exit ISMENE.

THESEUS
Madam, your colour changes and you appear
tongue-tied. What was Hippolytus doing here?

ARICIA
He came to say goodbye.

THESEUS
Apparently
your eyes have tamed that savage spirit
and put a pulse into that stony heart.

ARICIA
I don't deny it; your son didn't inherit
your adversarial attitude toward myself.
He hasn't treated me like a common thief.

THESEUS
No doubt he's sworn eternal love; however
I wouldn't rely on such an inconstant lover.
He's sworn as much to others.

ARICIA
Really?

Oh yes; you should have taught him some discretion.
How can you choose this base affiliation?

ARICIA
How can you let these calumnies destroy
the brilliant future of your eldest boy?
Have you so little knowledge of his heart?
Can't you tell guilt and innocence apart?
Some dark cloud hides from your eyes alone
the integrity for which your son is known.
Would you deliver him into scheming hands?
You must retract your homicidal words
and tremble lest the literal-minded gods
hate you so much they meet your harsh demands.
Too often they accept our sacrifices;
their gifts are often punishments for our vices.

THESEUS
You needn't try to excuse his misbehaviour.
Your love blinds you, clearly, in his favour;
but I have evidence, irrefutable proof —
for me, Phaedra's tears are more than enough.

ARICIA
Be careful, sir. We know you've cleared these lands
of countless monsters with your own bare hands,
but not all are destroyed; there's one . . .
But your own son forbids me to go on.
Knowing the great respect he has for you,
I'll only injure him if I continue;
so I shall imitate his reticence
and leave you now, lest I should break my silence.

Exit ARICIA.

THESEUS
What is she driving at? What does she mean
by these half-finished sentences, broken off, re-begun?
Are they trying to pull the wool over my eyes?

Are they in league to torture me with lies?
And I myself, despite my self-control,
what faint whisper screams in my very soul?
A vague compunction pains and unnerves me.
I need to sound Oenone one more time
and get more light on this mysterious crime.

Enter PANOPE.

PANOPE
My lord, the queen clearly intends to die —
her mind is in a kind of terminal chaos.
Mortal despair is evident in her face,
which is as white as death. Meanwhile Oenone
has drowned herself from the cliffs at Navarone
for no earthly reason that we can see;
her secret lies with her beneath the sea.

THESEUS
Oenone drowned?

PANOPE
Her suicide
exacerbates the queen's frenzy, I'm afraid.
From time to time, in her delirium,
she clasps her children and weeps over them;
and then, as if renouncing human love,
she thrusts them from her with a violent shove.
She wanders aimlessly about the place;
her vacant gaze seems not to recognize us.
Thrice now she has sat down to write; and thrice
she has ripped up the unfinished letter. Sir,
see her, I beg you; try to comfort her.

THESEUS
Oenone dead, and Phaedra bent on death?
Where is my son? Let him defend himself!
Let him speak; I'm ready to hear him now.
Poseidon, wait, I here revoke my vow!
Oh, let it not be heard!

I was too quick to turn to you.
What slanderous tongues have I been listening to?
What devastation if my prayer is answered!

Enter THERAMENES.

Theramenes, is that you? Where is your pupil?

THERAMENES
Sir, your solicitude is admirable
but comes too late.

THESEUS
Oh, God!

THERAMENES
I've watched
the most agreeable of men dispatched
and, dare I say it, the least culpable.

THESEUS
The very minute I reach out to him
the impatient gods decide his hour has come!
Say it was quick; did lightning strike him down?

THERAMENES
We'd scarcely left the outskirts of the town.
He drove his chariot — his unhappy men,
as silent as himself, riding behind.
Grimly we set out on the Mycenae road,
the reins slack in his distracted hand.
I watched his noble hunters, once so proud
and eager to obey his brisk command,
who now, with lowered head and mournful eye,
seemed to adapt their gait to his own reverie.
All of a sudden a gut-wrenching roar
from the sea's depths shocked the silent air
and a loud voice from deep under the ground
groaned in reply. The blood froze in our veins,
the coarse hair bristled in the horses' manes;

61

and then there rose, upon the level calm,
dimming the sun, a boiling cliff of foam
which, crashing swiftly toward the shaken land,
spewed up a monster on the burning sand,
its huge head crowned with enormous horns,
its body clothed in pale, malodorous scales —
half bull, half dragon, fiery and determined,
its tail thrashing in labyrinthine coils.
With a prolonged roar it shook the shore
while the sky seemed to watch in fear;
the earth moved and a foul stench filled the air,
the wave that bore it in recoiled in terror.
Since it seemed pointless to resist, we ran
and hid in the ruined shrine behind the strand —
except Hippolytus, your heroic son,
who reined his chariot, seized a javelin,
went for the monster and, at the first cast,
opened a large wound in the furious beast.
Dripping with slime, writhing in pain and rage,
it fell down howling at the water's edge,
rolled over, opened up a fiery mouth
and choked the horses with its blood and smoke
so that they fled in panic with the youth,
insensible alike to rein or voice,
while the valiant prince struggled to check their flight
and the bits bubbled with a bloody froth.
Some claim to have glimpsed, amid the sulphurous noise,
the god Poseidon goading neck and back
so that their terror drove them on a rock
where the fast-whirring axle screamed and broke.
The shattered chariot smashed in glittering splinters
and fragments flew, while the unfortunate prince
fell tangled in the reins. Oh, what a sight!
I can't erase the picture from my mind
of your son dragged over the jaggèd ground
by the same horses he had fed and trained.
He called on them to stop, but his frantic voice
only increased their panic; on they flew,
bashing his brains and bones on the rocks below,
their hooves slamming into his upturned face

till the hills echoed to our cries of woe.
At length the frenzied dash drew to a close;
the horses stopped beside the ancient shrine
of your ancestors, the princes of your line,
where, led by a trail of entrails in the crevices
and tufts of hair snagged on the thorn-bushes,
I scrambled down to him, the soldiers too,
and murmured something. Reaching out in pain,
he looked up once and closed his eyes again.
'The gods have claimed my innocent life,' he said;
'take care of poor Aricia when I'm dead;
and if, one day, my father, disabused,
mourns an unhappy son falsely accused,
tell him he can appease my plaintive ghost
by treating her more kindly than in the past
and by restoring . . . ' With these words he died
and a disfigured corpse lay at my side —
a piteous victim of the harsh deities
whom not even you, my lord, would recognize.

THESEUS
Ah, son — the dear hope I myself destroyed!
Inexorable gods, too promptly you obeyed!
What agonies of remorse must I now feel?

Enter ARICIA *and* ISMENE.

THERAMENES
Just then the shy Aricia chanced along,
in flight from you and searching for your son
whom she had planned to wed in secret. Well,
she looked at the red sand and trampled bracken
and noticed, with a scared glance, Hippolytus
stretched out among the rocks, defaced and broken.
At first she couldn't face the obvious
and, failing to recognize the beloved youth,
stood staring at him and asking for him, both.
At length, acknowledging the awful truth,
she raised a bitter gaze of recognition
to pitiless heaven; then, shivering and spent,

collapsed beside her lover in a faint.
Ismene, sobbing, brought her back to life —
or rather, to a life of endless grief;
and I, my lord, have come, in my disgust,
to tell you of Hippolytus' last request
and so acquit myself of the grim trust
your son required of me with his dying breath.
But look, there stands the one responsible for his death!

Enter PHAEDRA.

THESEUS
You have your victory, my son is dead;
and yet I fear my own sneaking suspicion
which tells me he was innocent.
In any case he's dead, justly or no.
You may congratulate yourself on your achievement.
As for myself, I do not wish to know:
no doubt he was at fault if you say so.
His death is quite enough for me to bear
without examining the matter further —
which, while it couldn't bring him back to me,
might only aggravate my misery.
No, far from here and far from you, exiled
from Greece, I'll grieve for my dismembered child;
indeed, so insupportable is my woe,
I'd gladly leave behind the life we know.
My very fame sharpens my agony,
all eyes will know of my stupidity;
and how can a great king live like a solitary?
I now resent the honours showered on me
by barbarous deities; and I go
to mourn their murderous co-operation;
nor will I bore them with my prayers again.
Do what they will, they can't restore my son.

PHAEDRA
The time has come to break a guilty silence.
We must acknowledge your son's innocence;
he did no wrong.

THESEUS
Ah, Phaedra,
it was on your word I condemned him!
Oh, wickedness! Do you think your false report . . . ?

PHAEDRA
Theseus, listen to me, my time is short.
I was the impious and incestuous one
who cast a sinful eye on your chaste son.
The heavens struck fire into my hapless breast
and the perverse Oenone did the rest.
She feared the chaste prince, knowing my mad desire,
would tell the whole thing to his jealous father;
so, taking advantage of my great fatigue,
she rushed to charge him with a vile intrigue —
and paid the penalty; for, denounced by me,
she found too swift a death beneath the sea.
By now I would have perished by the sword
but that would have left the prince under a cloud;
and so, to make time for this full disclosure,
I've chosen a slower road to Acheron's shore
and drunk, to soothe my seething veins, a fierce
poison the witch Medea brought to Greece —
so that I feel, already, a strange frost
about my heart, and am at peace at last.
I see the heavens only as through a mist
where my wronged spouse dissolves into a ghost
while death, dimming my vision, mercifully
restores to the light its tarnished purity.

PANOPE
She's dead, sir.

THESEUS
Would to God the thought
of her dark deeds might die with her!
Come now, my friends, now that the facts are known,
let's mix our tears with the blood of my dead son,
honour his corpse, expiate my demented prayer,
recall those qualities we cherished most;

and, further to appease his querulous ghost,
Aricia I declare,
despite our differences, my daughter and my heir.